Women of the Klan
Foundations of Modern Feminism

John Davis, BA., J.D., LL.M.

Old Town Industries, Inc.
1978   Old Town Publishing

ISBN: 1507710933

ISBN-13: 978-1507710937

DEDICATION

This monograph is dedicated to all who work with victims of prejudice and bigotry, those who tirelessly strive for equality based upon race, gender or creed, and those who have, through the struggles of the civil rights movements in the United States, left an indelible mark on the progress of freedom, liberty and egalitarianism.

Jus Gentium: omnes homines naturâ æquales sunt.

"Four score, and seven years ago, our Fathers brought forth onto *this* continent, a *new* nation conceived in liberty, and dedicated to the proposition: *: omnes homines naturâ æquales sunt. . . ."*

It is all together fitting and proper that we should do this, that these honorèd dead shall not have died in vain . . . . and that the *Jus Gentium* shall not perish from the Earth."

President Abraham Lincoln
Gettysburg Address – November 19, 1863

"Beneath this Flag that waves above,
This cross that lights our way,
You'll always find a sister's love,
In the heart of each Tri-K"

Ritual of the Tri-K Klub (Tri-K Klub of the Women of the Ku Klux Klan, 1925), 16. Kathleen M. Blee. Women of the Klan: Racism and Gender in the 1920s (Kindle Location 2814). Kindle Edition.

Figure 1 – Power March of the Women's Klan – Washington D.C. (1928) At the peak of the Ku Klux Klan's power in 1925, there were over 500,000 Women members of "The Invisible Empire." The Klan, or KKK, sought to advance women's voting, among other women's interests, to dilute the power of the vote that Washington, D.C. had extended to Afro-American men under the Fifteenth Amendment to the U.S. Constitution.

ACKNOWLEDGMENTS

The Author and Publisher would like to thank Prentice Reid, and Chandrapal S. Bhasker, for their insights into the shadowy recesses of those who would exploit men of peace.

Table of Contents

WOMEN OF THE KLAN
FOUNDATIONS OF MODERN FEMINISM

John Davis[1]

The invisible Empire – Women of the Klan

The stereotype of members of the Ku Klux Klan, is of a rural Southern white man who commits random acts of terror and violence against Catholics and African-Americans.

However, almost unknown to the American

---

[1] *Bacheloris Artis*, Case Western Reserve University 1975; *Juris Doctor*, Seattle University School of Law 1981; *Legis Magister*, New York University School of Law 1984.

public, and the world, was a vast organization of Women who subscribed to the values of the Ku Klux Klan, and, who used the sometimes violent arm of the men of the Ku Klux Klan, to promote their agenda for women's suffrage, temperance, and women's supremacy.

These women, numbering in the hundreds of thousands, comprised what was known as "the invisible empire."

The Ku Klux Klan is out of politics henceforth and will carry on work of an "invisible" nature hereafter, according to Mrs. Robie Gill Comer, imperial commander of the women of the Klan. This picture of her was taken in Indianapolis, where 25,000 Klanswomen gathered for a jubilee convention.

The invisible empire, though virtually an almost secret organization, was responsible for much of the ability of the Ku Klux Klan [KKK], to infiltrate the legitimate government bodies of state and federal governments in the U.S. The agendas of the Women's KKK seemed benign – they were ostensibly seeking "equality" with men (in all matters) – the removal of Eurocentric traditions that they believed limited women's roles in society, and they were seeking values which encouraged a matriarchy to re-build the families that had been ravaged and devastated by war (specifically the Civil War).

CREED OF KLANSWOMEN

WE BELIEVE in the American home as the foundation upon which rests secure the American Republic, the future of its institutions, and the liberties of its citizens.

WE BELIEVE in the mission of emancipated womanhood, freed from the shackles of old-world traditions, and standing unafraid in the full effulgence of equality and enlightenment.

WE BELIEVE in the equality of men and women in political, religious, fraternal, civic and social affairs wherein there should be no distinction of sex.

In fact, the Invisible Empire had the exact same ostensible goals of 19th century feminism – an androgynous "equality" between men and women (in which women were superior and men were disposable).

Unfortunately, however, what the KKK promoted as benign objectives, around lofty and noble images of "equality" was, as modern feminism itself, merely a disguise for gender supremacy.

Figure 2 - The ostensible purposes of the Invisible Empire - women of the Klan - was complete "equality" between men and women, in which women held a sanctimonious role of being superior to men.

In the cold light of history, what emerged from the Women of the Klan, was a pattern of exclusivity and supremacy, especially towards African-American Men and Catholic Men (specifically Hispanic men). It is a pattern that continues, today, in the realities of modern feminism and its pervasive influence over government, media and social constructs.

In her doctoral thesis, Dr. Sarah Elizabeth Doherty, of Loyola University Chicago, has uncovered the real agenda of Women of the Klan, and their pervasive influence within the Ku Klux Klan itself. In her work: "Aliens Found in Waiting: Women of the Ku Klux Klan in Suburban Chicago, 1870-1930: [Women of the Klan deemed anyone who was not a member of the Klan to be an "*alien.*"]

The KKK never resolved gender issues that were complicated by female sympathizers seeking a more active role in Klan activities. Rhetoric of the Reconstruction-era Klan called upon white Protestant men to protect and guard the virtue of white womanhood against the threat of freed slaves and carpetbaggers from the North. The language in 1920s Klan publications, in terms of women, focused on the importance of motherhood and the duty of Protestant women to promote the ideals of American citizenry as interpreted by the Ku Klux Klan. Female supporters of the Klan were active in social movements such as suffrage and temperance and became accustomed to involvement outside the home in clubs and organizations.12 Though Klan officials wanted to find a place for women within the Invisible Empire, they envisioned women in an auxiliary subordinate role. By the time serious consideration was given to the creation of a women's division of the KKK, many women's organizations with related creeds and agendas to the men's Klan already existed. Similar purposed groups included the Ladies of the Cu Clux Clan, Ladies of the Golden Den, Ladies of the Golden Mask, Queens of the Golden Mask, Ladies of the Invisible Eye, Kamelia, Grand League of Protestant Women, Order of American Women, Dixie Protestant Women's Political League, Hooded Ladies of the Mystic Den, Women's Krudaders, Puritan Daughters of America and Ladies of the Invisible Empire or "Loties."13 Klan leadership favored the creation of a new women's organization to be called the Women of the Ku Klux Klan to cooperate with and complement the mission of the men's order.14²

---

² Footnotes reproduced here from original thesis: [11] Baker, Gospel

However, behind the mask of "chivalry" and "equality," in step with the main branches of the Ku Klux Klan, the women of the Invisible Empire sought to use brutality, intimidation, lynchings, cross-burnings, torture and political corruption perpetrated by the Klan's "Ghouls" and "White Knights." The "Ghouls" and "White Knights" of the Klan, much like male feminists today, enabled the Women of the Klan to seek power over men, in society, especially men who were not "White Protestants."

(Among other facets of modern society, we have only to look at the huge numbers of African-American men imprisoned in the United States, today, to understand that the Invisible Empire, over a period of a century and a half, has succeeded, with feminism, in demonizing African-American men, in particular, and men in general).

One learned treatise on Women in the Klan,

According to the Klan, 136-39. [12] See Blee, "Joining the Ladies' Organization" in Women of the Ku Klux Klan, 101-22. [13] Ibid, 25-7. [14] "Report of Women of the Ku Klux Klan" [c. 1924], 110-13, Collections of the Indiana Historical Society.

explains the real purpose behind the "Invisible Empire." In "Women of the Klan: Racism and Gender in the 1920's," noted feminist author Kathleen M. Blee writes:

> *For thousands of native-born white Protestant women . . . , the women's Klan of the 1920s was not only a way to promote racist, intolerant, and xenophobic policies but also a social setting in which to enjoy their own racial and religious privileges. These women recall their membership in one of U.S. history's most vicious campaigns of prejudice and hatred primarily as a time of friendship and solidarity among like-minded women. But the Klan's appeal to this Indiana woman was not based purely on racism and nativism.*
>
> *In an effort to recruit members among women newly enfranchised in the 1920s, the Klan also insisted that it was the best guarantor of white Protestant women's rights. The political efforts of a women's order, the Klan claimed, could safeguard women's suffrage and expand women's other legal rights while working to preserve white Protestant supremacy.* [3]

(One has only to look at the well-documented and vitriolic campaign of modern feminism, against Catholicism, and the Catholic Church,

---

[3] Kathleen M. Blee, Women of the Klan: Racism and Gender in the 1920s (Kindle Locations 37-39). Kindle Edition.

and Men's equality organizations, to understand that modern feminism is merely the extension of the "Invisible Empire" into the 21st Century).

Figure 3 - Feminists of the group "FEMEN" appear at the Vatican to express their hatred for Catholics and Catholicism. This tactic is similar to the repulsive and ostentatious tactics of the anti-Catholic KKK.

This book explores the parallels between the Invisible Empire and modern feminism, and shows how modern feminism is an extension of the principles of the Ku Klux Klan, its supremacy and exclusivity, and its pattern of using violence against men, disguised as "justice," to invalidate real notions of "equality" between men and women.

Early History of Gynocentric[4] Chivalry and the Klan

The name "Ku Klux Klan" derives from the Attic Greek concept of κύκλος (pronounced: koó-klos, hence koó-klos clan or KKK). Literally, κύκλος means "cycle." It refers to the concepts of a cycle of governance that was identified by Plato in "The Republic" in Chapters VIII and IX. In Pla-

---

[4] *Gynocentric,* Syllabification: gy·no·cen·tric ADJECTIVE: Centered on or concerned exclusively with women; taking a female (or specifically a feminist) point of view. Oxford English Dictionary (2014).

to's view, the cycle of governance begins with democracy, and inevitably degenerates into oligarchy, then tyranny.[5]

Immediately after the immense tragedy of the American Civil War, the defeated South viewed the government in Washington, D.C., under President Abraham Lincoln, as a tyranny.

In response to that perceived tyranny, Southerners, on December 24, 1865, gathered in a law office in Pulaski, Tennessee, to form the KKK.

---

[5] But see, Doherty, Sarah Elizabeth, "Aliens Found in Waiting: Women of the Ku Klux Klan in Suburban Chicago, 1870-1930, doctoral thesis, Loyola University (2012). "The name was derived from the corruption of the Greek word "kukloi" or "kuklos" meaning a band or circle of brotherhood. The Klan portion of the name was added later for effect and spelled with a "k" for uniformity. Another theory for the origins of the name is that it was derived from the name of the Aztec Mexican "god of light" or "Cukulan." 30,000 men from Tennessee volunteered for the Mexican War and were feasibly exposed to ancient Aztec folklore and culture. The "knights" portion of the name was later added to accompany the imagery of crusading knights printed on Klan propaganda pamphlets and tracts."

Figure 4 - The actual building at which the KKK was formed on Christmas Eve, 1865, in Pulaski, Tennessee

An account of the formation of the organization is contained in a very rare manuscript known as "The Authentic History of the Ku Klux Klan" by Susan Lawrence Davis (1924). Ms. Davis recounts the actual formation of the KKK in her semi-autobiographical account. Ms. Davis was an eye-witness to the formation of the Klan.

During the evening the organization was perfected. Captain John B. Kennedy, on the committee to select a name mentioned one which he had considered, "Kukloi," from the Greek word "Kuklos," meaning a band or circle. James R. Crowe said "Call it Ku Klux," and no one will know what it means. John C. Lester said: "Add Klan as we are all Scotch-Irish de-

scent."

He then repeated the words: "Ku Klux Klan," the first time these words ever fell from human tongue. The weirdness of the alliteration appealed to the mysterious within them; so the name was adopted with a feeling that they had chosen something which would excite the curiosity of their friends and carry out their idea of amusement, which, most unexpectedly to them, proved a boon to Pulaski and the South.

James R. Crowe suggested to make it more mysterious, that a costume be adopted. They then made a raid upon Mrs. Martin's linen closet and robed themselves with boyish glee in her stiff linen sheets and pillow-cases, as masquerading was a popular form of entertainment in those days. Wishing to make an impression they borrowed some horses from a nearby stable and disguised them with sheets.

The precepts of the Ku Klux Klan (KKK) are clear in its originating documents promulgated in 1868. The KKK ". . . is an institution of chivalry . . . . embodying in its genius and its principles all that is chivalric . . . ." [*Id.*]

But what did the founders of the KKK consider to be "chivalry?"

To answer that question, it is necessary to reach into the past about 1,000 years.

Chivalry began roughly around the turn of the first millennium (about 1,000 A.D.). Not coincidentally, this time period saw a large amount of hyper-aggression among European feudal lords, seeking to increase their power, wealth and military influences. These same feudal lords, some pretending to be kings and emperors, sought excuses to enter the crusades for the ostensible purpose of reclaiming the Holy Lands from Islam. In reality, however, their purpose was to increase their ability to plunder neighboring kingdoms, Middle Eastern civilizations, and increase their stores of gold and slaves.

It is during this period of slavery, hyper-aggression, militarism, plunder and incessant feudal conflicts, that the Klan's notions of "chivalry" evolved into what it was at the turn of the 20th Century in the U.S.

Feudal chivalry was marked by one distinguishable characteristic. Men were considered disposable, in combat or otherwise, in the service of women, who were elevated to a special sanctity and protected status. (Not unlike their status under modern feminism).

The turn of the first millennium saw a change in European culture's views of women. With the assistance of the Church, women were elevated to a special status because of their abilities to give birth (to replenish the supply of soldiers (cannon fodder) needed for feudalism), and, as being necessary to provide heirs to thrones and feudal holdings.

Below is a diagram of the process by which women underwent a positive re-evaluation of what Charlemagne's court would term: *La querelle des femmes* ("the question of women" [and their role in society]). Women's roles, as a collective gender, evolved from being mostly slaves (owned, like men, by the state) to a new level of sanctity requiring the solicitous chivalry and gallantry of men for their protection and succor.

Men were relegated to their roles as disposable defenders of the realm, and, the women who ruled over the realm.

Feudalism created a structure of "civilization" in which men were given grandiose titles, and lofty positions of supposed power. This gave the illusion that men were the ones who controlled civilization. The reality of feudalism, however, was that men were pledged from birth to be in service of women; women retained the right to life and to be "defended" at the expense of the lives of men; and women retained more powers over property, civil discourse and sexuality, while they were safe at home than the men being slaughtered on the battlefields.

Figure 6 – (tapestry) Eleanor of Aquitaine as leader of the Second Crusade (in which hundreds of thousands of men died to increase her power and wealth).

This became clear during the reign(s) of Eleanor of Aquitaine.

Eleanor of Aquitaine (1137-1152) was one of the most powerful and influential figures of the Middle Ages. Inheriting a vast estate at the age of 15 made her the most sought-after bride of her generation. She would eventually become the queen of France, the queen of England and lead a crusade to the Holy Land. She is also credited with establishing and preserving many of the courtly rituals of chivalry.[6]

[6] http://www.history.com/topics/british-history/eleanor-of-

The 12th century intersection of cultural factors that created the gynocentric cultural complex (GCC) and subsequent timeline of events

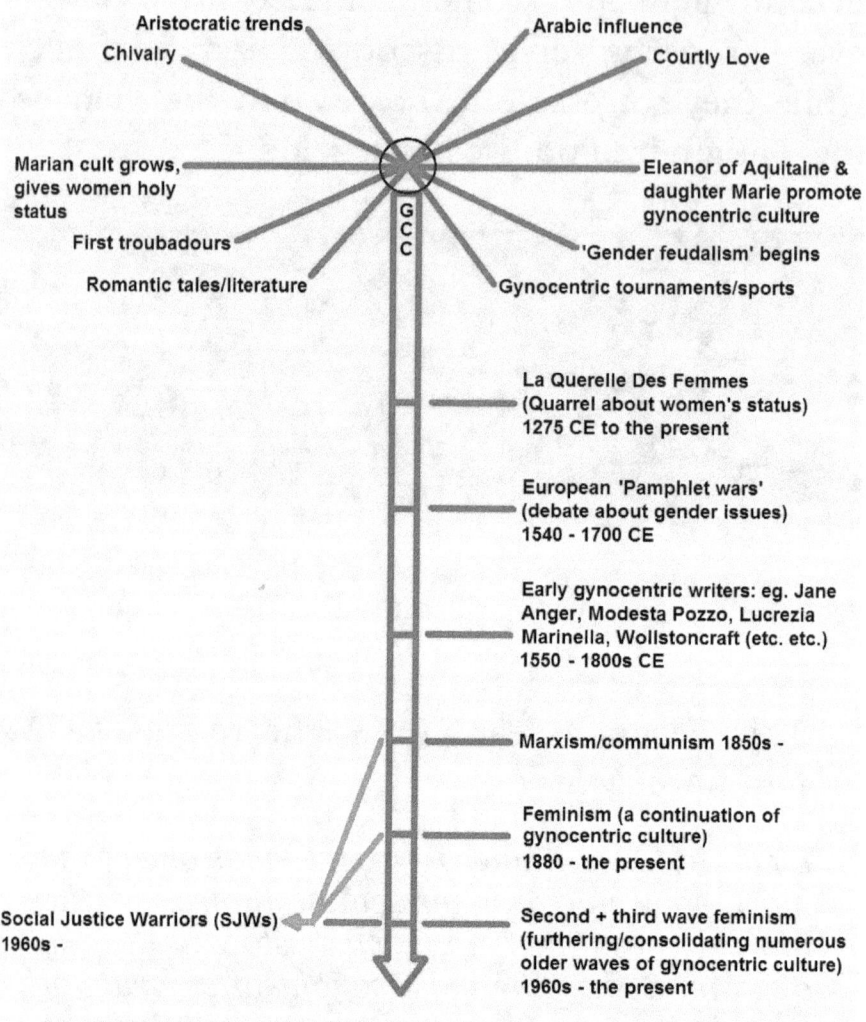

Aristocratic trends

Chivalry

Arabic influence

Courtly Love

Marian cult grows, gives women holy status

Eleanor of Aquitaine & daughter Marie promote gynocentric culture

First troubadours

'Gender feudalism' begins

Romantic tales/literature

Gynocentric tournaments/sports

GCC

La Querelle Des Femmes (Quarrel about women's status) 1275 CE to the present

European 'Pamphlet wars' (debate about gender issues) 1540 - 1700 CE

Early gynocentric writers: eg. Jane Anger, Modesta Pozzo, Lucrezia Marinella, Wollstoncraft (etc. etc.) 1550 - 1800s CE

Marxism/communism 1850s -

Feminism (a continuation of gynocentric culture) 1880 - the present

Social Justice Warriors (SJWs) 1960s -

Second + third wave feminism (furthering/consolidating numerous older waves of gynocentric culture) 1960s - the present

Figure 7 – The creation of the Gynocentric Cultural Complex (GCC). Diagram courtesy of: Peter Wright.

aquitaine

"Courtly rituals of chivalry" refers to an actual court system, presided over by Eleanor of Aquitaine herself, her daughter Marie . . . and sixty other women (but not a single man). They were known as *"les cours d'amour"* - "The Courts of Love."

This amounted to little more than state-sponsored feminism. In this "court" system, Eleanor, a woman, and sixty other women were the sole arbiters of customs between men and women engaged in intimacy.

If a woman felt aggrieved by her lover, she would bring her complaint to the Court and either Eleanor, or Marie, or other high-born women would "resolve" the dispute. The queen's resolutions were enforceable by means of the queen's command over state violence. They were also enforceable through severe social sanctions such as shunning.

In addition, literary poets and troubadours of the time, spread gynocentric viewpoints of the powerful Queen Eleanor all across Europe. The literary poets and troubadours were the "mainstream media" of the time. The gynocentric judgments of *les cours d'amour* (the courts of love), coupled with Eleanor's political power as

Queen of both France and England, insured that the gynocentric attitudes of the Poitevin Code [the courts of love were located in Poitiers in the South of France] became the law and the prevailing gender attitudes across most of Europe.

What were the codes of the courts of love? The most accurate statement comes from a scholar writing in 1937 in a well-respected journal article. Writing in Speculum: A Journal of Mediaeval Studies (January, 1937), Amy Kelly writes:

"In the Poitevin code, man is the **property**, the very **thing** of woman. . . ."[7]

Chivalry, therefore, had little or nothing to do with equality between men and women. Chivalry became modern feminism, in which men are merely "disposable property and things," for women who want to "have it all."

This "Court of Love," and the Poitevin code, evolved over the ensuing 800 years into what we now know as the "system of family courts." Although there are many male judges presiding

---

[7] Kelly, Amy. "Eleanor of Aquitaine and Her Courts of Love." 12.1 SPECU-LUM: A JOURNAL OF MEDIEVAL STUDIES 14 (1937).

over our system of "family courts," those males have been subjected to 800 years of gynocentric conditioning and modern feminism. As a result, current "family courts" isolate most Fathers from their children, strip the Fathers of their assets and income (through alimony, property distributions and child support) and routinely seize children to be placed into the "foster home" or adoption system of the State pending the award of sole custody to the mother.

Nothing could be more pleasing to modern feminism than this wholesale destruction of the nuclear family by the state. To quote one modern feminist, Linda Gordon:

> *"The nuclear family must be destroyed, and people must find better ways of living together.... Whatever its ultimate meaning, the break-up of families now is an objectively revolutionary process....Families will be finally destroyed only when a revolutionary social and economic organization permits people's needs for love and security to be met in ways that do not impose divisions of labor, or any external roles, at all."*[8]

However noble chivalry may have been considered in medieval times, what is clear is that

---

[8] Linda Gordon, "Functions of the Family," Women: A Journal of Liberation (Fall 1969).

modern feminism has used the obligations men feel to be "chivalrous" in a way that imposes only burdens and responsibilities on men, and bestows lofty rights and privileges on women. The concept of chivalry has now evolved (or corrupted) to impose unwarranted and unnecessary privileges upon women, solely at the expense of men.

Writing in "The Fraud of Feminism" Ernst Belfort Bax wrote about the feminist view of chivalry:

It is plain then that chivalry as understood in the present day really spells sex privilege and sex favouritism pure and simple, and that any attempts to define the term on a larger basis, or to give it a colourable rationality founded on fact, are simply subterfuges, conscious or unconscious, on the part of those who put them forward. [9]

Although Bax wrote that epiphany over 100 years ago, it is still "spot on" today. Feminists refer to it as the "Chivalry Hypothesis." The chivalry hypothesis predicts that women will receive special, privileged treatment in societal

---

[9] Bax, Ernst Belfort, *The Fraud of Feminism*, Chapter V (The Chivalry Fake), London (1913).

constructs, while men will be relegated to positions of disposable convenience for society (some call it: "involuntary servitude."]

For example, men in the U.S. have less rights to vote than women. Under the U.S. Selective Service Act, each man, when he attains eighteen years of age, must register for the compulsory draft in the U.S. for compulsory military service. Women are exempt from this requirement. If men fail to register for compulsory military service, they are denied the right to vote. Outrageously, they are denied the right to apply for student loans, to obtain government financing, to work for the government, and are subjected to a host of other punishments from which their sisters are immune.

In the corrupt judicial system in the United States, there exist numerous sexist laws that deny men rights equal to women. None is more pronounced than the "Violence Against Women Act." This law was originally adopted in Congress (at the fanatical assistance of the now Vice President Joe Biden) to worship the myth that men who beat their wives are so common that a federal law was necessary to address the issue.

The result was atrocious discrimination against men. The Act requires to the police responding to an emergency call involving domestic violence to make an arrest if there is any evidence of violence against a woman. Although the law is conveniently worded so as, *"de jure"* [by law] the police should also arrest the women if there is any evidence of violence against the man, because of the myth of "wife beaters" and rank misandry in U. S. culture, 98% of the time there is mutual domestic violence, only the man is arrested and the woman is immune. This is known as *"de facto"* [in fact] discrimination – although the law, on its face, does not discriminate against men, the way the law is applied, in fact, is perniciously discriminatory against men.

These gynocentric constructs were exactly what were contemplated by early feminists, by modern feminists, and by the KKK.

By 1925, the KKK had openly adopted a feminist (gynocentric) agenda (stated in the archaic language of the time). For example, the 1925 manual of the KKK called for men who were "White Knights" to follow a code of gynocentric principals. "White Knights" were known as "Ghouls" and were not uncommonly charged by the KKK with lynching, torturing and brutalizing men at the mere accusation of women. In current paradigms, perhaps not coincidentally, men who "chivalrously" impose violence on other men to please women and feminists are known in common language as "White Knights." Not coincidentally, the ghouls of the Ku Klux Klan, who violently enforced the "chivalry" of the Klan upon the rest of the world in order to "defend" "virtuous womanhood."

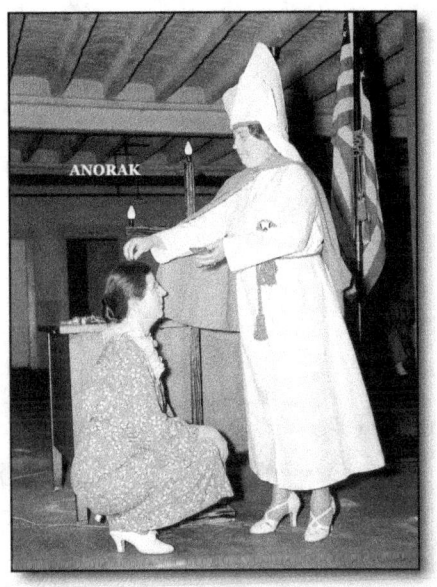

The modern "White Knights" include America's domestic police forces who are some of the most aggressive, militaristic, violent, racist, sexist, and misandrist organizations in the world.

The fierce directives of the Klan, to brutalize other men (especially Catholic men and African-American men) for the sake of "virtuous womanhood" were not unlike the current laws requiring police to make mandatory arrests of men in cases of mere accusations of domestic violence, or the current draconian actions of universities against male students who are merely accused of sexual misconduct, or, the media "lynch mobs" that destroy any man's character who is merely accused of sexual misconduct in our present day culture.

JOIN THE KKK
Loyal White Knights

Call Us Today (336)
www **com**
Loyal White Knights of the KKK

Figure 8 - "Ghouls" of the KKK who protect "virtuous womahood" are known as "White Knights" - men who support feminism are also known as "White Knights." Note the androgynous characteristic of the "White Knight" in the drawing.

The feminist principles the Klan imposed on its Ghouls included the following:

"It is the sworn duty of "the Ghouls" to serve as a chivalrous army for protecting 'noble womanhood' and that no one could rise above women."

"Womanhood. The Knights of the Ku Klux Klan declares that it is committed to "the sacred duty of protecting womanhood"; and announces that one of its purposes is "to shield . . . the chastity of womanhood."

"The degradation of women is a violation of the sacredness of human personality, a sin against the race, a crime against society, a menace to our country, and a prostitution of all that is best, and noblest, and highest in life. No race, or society, or country, can rise higher than its womanhood..."

Figure 9 – "No race, or society, or country, can rise higher than its womanhood..."

"11. Major Offenses [of Klan doctrines and precepts]

"Major offenses shall consist of...

3. "Disrespect of virtuous womanhood.""

Figure 10 - The Klan ideal of "virtuous womanhood." Note the absence of the Father of the child. It is characteristic of modern feminism to eliminate men from a "family" and alienate the Father from the family.

These exact precepts were, in fact, the same precepts promulgated by early suffragettes and feminists. They are the tenets of modern feminism in the 21st Century.

False Accusations of Rape:

Modern feminists, in a manner identical to their "sisters" in the 19th and 20th Century Ku Klux Klan, are intensely covetous of womyn's rights to falsely accuse a man . . . any man . . . of rape.

The horrific crime of rape, as feminists remind us, is not just about sex. It is about power.

Similarly, falsely accusing a man of rape is not just about sex . . . it is about power. It is about the power to accuse. It is about the power to raise the hatred and contempt of an entire society against one single man. It is about the power to hold public trials in the world-wide media. It is about the power to ruin a man's life, in the shade of the hanging tree, without due process.

A woman accusing a man of rape is the closest thing possible to a witch's curse, in which the mere utterance of words can bring complete ruin, torture and death upon any man the accuser wishes to destroy. A woman falsely accusing a man of rape is the feminist equivalent of rape itself.

For this reason, modern feminists closely guard their ability to falsely accuse men of rape. More than half of rape accusations in the United States are false accusations.

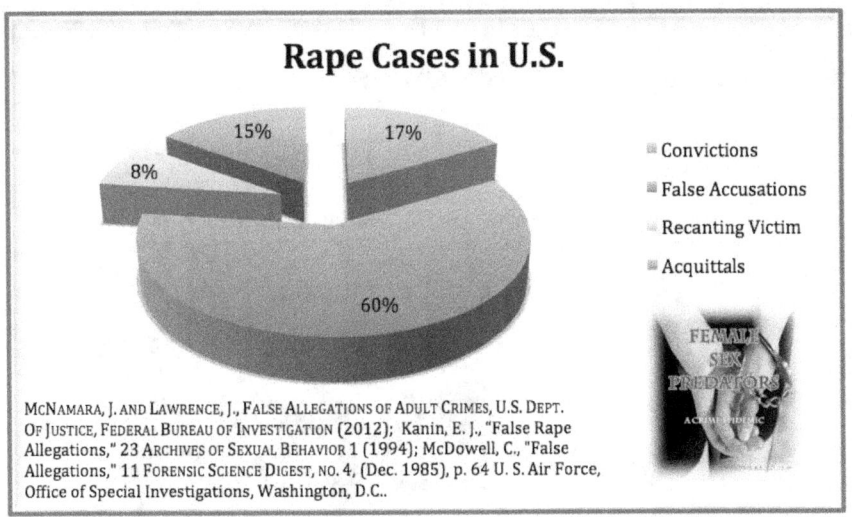

Rape Cases in U.S.

- Convictions
- False Accusations
- Recanting Victim
- Acquittals

17%
15%
8%
60%

McNamara, J. and Lawrence, J., False Allegations of Adult Crimes, U.S. Dept. of Justice, Federal Bureau of Investigation (2012); Kanin, E. J., "False Rape Allegations," 23 Archives of Sexual Behavior 1 (1994); McDowell, C., "False Allegations," 11 Forensic Science Digest, no. 4, (Dec. 1985), p. 64 U. S. Air Force, Office of Special Investigations, Washington, D.C..

Nevertheless, our gynocentric governments, legislators and police forces insist on giving women immunity for making false accusations of rape. The "reasoning" is that if the government punished women who made false accusations, it might deter women who are actually raped from coming forward.

This type of "reasoning" is like saying that we should not punish people who commit murder because it might result in the conviction of people who do not commit murder.

False accusations of rape have, in history, lead to lynchings, torture and tragedy. They continue to result in brutality and false prison sentences for innocent men, while women false

accusers are treated with "chivalry" and extended immunity for their crimes.

The crimes of false accusations of rape are a
direct result of the corrupt Klan values that are
adopted by the legal and judicial system, and
the mainstream media, in the U.S.

The Klan's pervasive view of chivalry favoring
women, and its corruption of our modern legal

system, is no more apparent than it is in the disparity of sentences that men receive in relation to women, for the same crimes.

Sentencing Disparities Between Men and Women

Michigan State University School of Law, and two independent feminist researchers, recently conducted studies on the sentences women receive in relation to the sentences that men receive.

Professor Sonja Starr of the University of Michigan School of Law, in her recent (2012) paper on gender sentencing disparities, has exposed the blatant racism and misandry in America's judicial system.

In "Estimating Gender Disparities in Federal Criminal Cases," [click on link] Professor Starr noted that in the federal court system, it is common for judges to sentence men prison for three times longer, on the average, than women, for the same crimes.

Figure 11 - Professor Sonja Starr - University of Michigan School of Law – "This paper assesses gender disparities in federal criminal cases. It finds large gender gaps favoring women throughout the sentence length distribution (averaging over 60%), conditional on arrest offense, criminal history, and other pre-charge observables. Female arrestees are also significantly likelier to avoid charges and convictions entirely, and twice as likely to avoid incarceration if convicted."

In a related paper, released just a few days after her paper on gender based sentencing disparities, Professor Starr also noted that African-American men, who comprise over 70% of the U.S. prison population, receive sentences almost five times greater than white women for the same crimes.[10]

---

[10] Starr, Sonja & Rehavit, Mari, "Racial Disparity in the Criminal Justice Process: Prosecutors, Judges, and the Effects of United States v. Booker," University of Michigan Law School Scholarship Repository, November 1, 2012.

The results of these studies are clear. The U.S. judicial system has adopted, "hook line and sinker" the racist and misandrist views of the Klan into the official policies and procedures of the judiciary in the U.S.

In the area of sex crimes, the same sentencing disparity exists.

In their paper in the journal FEMINIST CRIMI-

NOLOGY, Randa Embry and Phillip Lyons, two feminist researchers, came to the same conclusions as Professor Starr.

Writing in "Sex-Based Sentencing : Sentencing Discrepancies Between Male and Female Sex Offenders," 7 Feminist Criminology 146 (2012), Embry and Lyons again expose the blatant misandry and racism in our judicial system.

In the area of sex crimes, men receive 3 to 4 times longer prison sentences than women, for the same crimes. In addition, women often escape prison sentences for committing sex crimes, whereas prison sentences are almost mandatorily imposed on men, and, always imposed on African-American men.

Not coincidentally, these sentencing disparities favoring women in criminal sentencing is referred to, by feminists, as the "chivalry hypothesis." According to Embry & Lyons' paper:

> *The chivalry thesis, often referred to as paternalism, is similarly situated. This model maps onto the traditional gender roles of men and women asserting that women are weaker and their actions are not seen as completely valid and almost "childlike." Thus, women should not be held to the same standards as men in the criminal justice system as they are not "fully responsible for their actions" (Rodriguez et al.,*

2006, p. 320).

These gender based sentencing disparities are the direct result of the judges in the U.S. adopting a century of Klan chivalry towards women, and, the feminist misandry and racism of those feminist leaders of the 19th and 20th centuries.

At least two prominent leaders of the "Women's Movement," after the civil war, were blatantly misandrist, and racist, and subscribed to Klan principles. These women were among influential national leaders who influenced the government of the U.S. to adopt hatred of men, and specifically hatred of black men, as official policy of the U.S. Government and its system of judges.

Elizabeth Cady Stanton: "Women are infinitely superior to men."

Elizabeth Cady Stanton, and the honored Susan B. Anthony, publicly demeaned prominent African-American men such as Frederick

Douglass.   Elizabeth Cady Stanton is often quoted by modern feminists as having said:

"Women are infinitely superior to men."

Figure 12 - Stanton disparaged black men and opposed giving African-American men the vote. She was quoted as saying "Women are infinitely superior to men." Much like modern feminism, she was both racist and misandrist.

Stanton and Susan B. Anthony (honored on a U.S. dollar coin) both openly opposed giving African-American men the vote after the civil war. They openly disparaged men and African-

Americans, and formed the National Women's Suffrage Association [NWSA] in 1869.

The NWSA was radical and, at times, terroristic in its approach to disparaging men. Though it was not directly related to the Ku Klux Klan, many of its objectives were identical to the Klan in terms of denying African-American men the right to vote, and, in disparaging men in general.

Relentless in their attacks on men, Anthony and Stanton became known as "The Belligerent Sisterhood."

In addition to being openly racist and misandrist, Stanton was also openly androphobic. "Women, Stanton said, must not put her trust in man."[11]

We must keep in mind that modern feminism considers these women, who were misandrist, androphobic and racist, to be the heroines of feminism, and among its founders. It is not surprising, therefore, to find modern feminism, disguised in politically correct euphemisms, to continue the racist, misandrist and androphobic attitudes and objectives of early suffragettes and

---

[11] Elizabeth Cady Stanton, qtd. In E. Forner at 115.

the Women of the Ku Klux Klan.

Margaret Sanger – Feminsim, Racism & Misandry

> "We do not want word to go out that we want to exterminate the Negro population, and the minister is the man who can straighten out that idea if it ever occurs to any of their more rebellious members. [Explaining rationale for using prominent black leaders to advocate birth control and abortion]"   - Margaret Sanger - 1923

Margaret Sanger is one of the heroines of feminism. She devoted her entire life to the establishment and perpetuation of planned parenthood, and, was the founder of Planned Parenthood.

Sanger's campaign to provide women "choice" in matters of procreation was a thinly veiled crusade to use modern science to control the race, national cultural characteristics and gender of civilization. Her dream included the specious nobility of providing women "choice," but, at the same time, included the nightmare of excluding men (especially Catholic immigrants (Hispanics and Irish)) from surviving "choice."

Figure 13 - "I accepted an invitation to talk to the women's branch of the Ku Klux Klan...I saw through the door dim figures parading with banners and illuminated crosses...I was escorted to the platform, was introduced, and began to speak...In the end, through simple illustrations I believed I had accomplished my purpose. A dozen invitations to speak to similar groups were proffered."
Margaret Sanger – autobiography.

Sanger's view of men was that they had no purpose in a family other than to assume the disposable role of provider. She also advocated that men should have no role in the decision-making process of family planning. Modern feminism holds this same misandry as one of its principal tenets. Like feminism, and the KKK, Sanger preached exclusivity in which women were elevated to sanctimonious status, while men were relegated to disposable functions in the concept of "family" and in the designs of the State.

Sanger's view of men in the reproductive process was deprecating to say the least. "Woman must have her freedom, the fundamental freedom of choosing whether or not she will be a mother and how many children she will have. Regardless of what man's attitude may be, that problem is hers — and before it can be his, it is hers alone."

Her misandrist and racist views spread quickly across the continent after, World War I, and she often resorted to alliance with the Ku Klux Klan in order to advance her feminist principles.

Modern feminism has adopted the misandry of Sanger and the KKK in grandiose terms:

"So, how do we control men's fertility? Mandatory contraception beginning at puberty, with the rule relaxed only for procreation under the right circumstances (he can afford it and has a willing partner) and for the right reasons (determined by a panel of experts, and with the permission of his designated female partner)."

"...controlling men's fertility would not be a

hard restriction to enforce. The fertility author-
ities could use a combination of punishments
for men who failed to get the implants and for
doctors who removed them without proper au-
thorization. The men could be required to
adopt one orphan per infraction and rear her
or him until adulthood. The doctors, could lose
their licenses or, in extreme cases, go to pris-
on."

One might be tempted to presume that this quote was of a fanatical fascist, pronouncing 19th century imperial views on social engineering.

This quote is from a 1997 article in Ms. Magazine, and was written by a modern feminist by the name of Margaret Burk.

Sanger's hatred of men, and her pervasive misandry, is no more apparent than in her own writings. In Chapter XVIII of her book: "Woman and the New Race," Sanger writes:

In all of the animal species below the human, motherhood has a clearly discernible superiority over fatherhood. It is the first pulse of organic life. Fatherhood is the fertilizing element. Its development, compared to that of the mother cell, is comparatively new. Likewise, its influence upon the progeny is comparatively small.

Translated into modern terms, Sanger is saying that men have no role in the human race other than to perform perfunctory fertilization. A reading of her book makes it clear that she views this as a valid premise for denying men any meaningful participation in the reproductive process of humans.

Sanger was a key in the early feminist movement to create a society in which men had no rights, and, in which White Women had no responsibilities. It was a vision that Sanger and early Feminism both shared to create a privileged class of White Women that enjoyed all of the benefits of society without having to contribute anything to society.

Women were a pervasive influence in the Ku Klux Klan. They molded its policy to conform to 19th century feminist views. By proxy, they used the terror and violence of KKK ghouls as "White Knights" to further their violent agendas against men and African-Americans.

In the 20th century, as the power of the Jim Crow era subsided in the U.S., feminists made it certain that the misandry (man-hating), and racism, of women in the Klan became a pervasive and acceptable official policy of the U.S. Government, its judicial system, and many other governments around the world.

Modern "Jim Crow:" – The "iHollaback" Initiative

The term "Jim Crow" refers to a system of enforcing segregation and racism in the U.S. South from the era of the Civil war, to approximately the presidency of John F. Kennedy in the 1960's.

James R. Crow (hence: "Jim Crow") was one of the original founders of the Ku Klux Klan in 1865. Through his influence in the widespread KKK activities of the time, he instituted a set of cultural norms, and corruption of the legal system across the United States, which was intended to keep African-Americans (and other minorities) in a subservient role similar to slavery in the South.

Modern feminism, under the pretense of womyn's "equality," is constantly attempting to institute a new "Jim Crow" system across the United States, and the world. The new feminist "Jim Crow" system would focus on the racism of the Klan, against minority men, but would be used to pass laws structured in such a way that they could entrap any male, and subject those men to arbitrary laws – laws that compel men to be subservient to women.

A classic example is the contemporary feminist drive to make it illegal for men to address a woman, in any manner, while she is in public.

This is known as the "*iHollaback*" initiative. The *iHollaback* initiative is a thinly disguised program of apartheid, segregation, racism and misandry.

In the autumn of 2014, for the purpose of raising donations, iHollaback created a heavily edited video of a frumpish white woman walking through Harlem in a tight T-shirt, displaying her breasts in a salacious manner. The video was shot only from a front perspective so that viewers could not see the prominent display of her breasts to the minority men in Harlem, or, the tightness of her jeans also displayed to the minority men.

After walking for ten hours, and being filmed, only from the front, the producers claimed that the woman (Shoshana Roberts) had accumulated over 100 incidences of street harassment from men. The remarks included salutations such as: "smile," "have a nice day," how you doing today?," God bless you mami," "you don't wanna talk?," and other common forms of addressing strangers in public.

Figure 14 – Shoshanna Roberts prominently displaying her breasts in a tight t-shirt, and her hips in tight jeans, soliciting remarks from minority men in Harlem, in order to "prove"

that men routinely harass women, and, therefore, should be subjected to criminal sanctions merely for speaking to her.

Many of the remarks that the producers claimed the men had made sounded as if they had been edited into the film as opposed to being actual remarks. In some cases, remarks were edited into the film at points in the film before the men, whom the producers claimed made remarks, could possibly have seen the woman in the film.

One woman commentator, Janet Bloomfield, described her manner in the film as "prissy." Prissy (and arrogant) is a fair description of the woman's demeanor in the film. As any resident of Manhattan is aware, such prissy and arrogant behavior, in most public settings, is likely to draw attention and solicit remarks from strangers.

By now, I am sure you have seen this video of a prissy white woman walking the "streets" of New York for 10 hours and being subjected to "harassment". Those words are in quotations because it turns out that the majority of the people saying hello and other inanities took place on one street in Harlem. Princess has rightly been called out for racism and hysteria, forcing iHollaback to issue an apology. "Gee we had no idea targeting men of color would make us look racist". Oh whatever. Nice back-pedal there, assholes.

I've written about street harassment before, specifically from the racism angle but today I want to talk about something bigger than just the racial element, although that's still a big part of it. What the iHollaback video, and indeed the entire organization and all that is represents does is contribute to a climate of fear. And not just run of mill, my Spidey senses went on alert fear, but full on hysterical, run away screaming fear.

Fear of what?

Of men. And of black men in particular.[12]

This type of fear is known as "androphobia."

Androphobia is common among feminists and results from cultural conditioning in misandry and racism. It is defined as:

androphobia
an-dro-pho-bi-a   Mor-
bid fear of men, including coming in contact, engaging in activities or becoming intimate with men.[13]

---

[12] http://judgybitch.com/2014/11/10/lets-talk-about-street-harassment/ ["The radical notion that women are adults."]

[13] file://localhost/<a href="http/::medical diction-ary.thefreedictionary.com:androphobia">androphobia<:a>

It is iHollaback's intended, and admitted, purpose to instill androphobia in the public in order to raise money, and to provide laws making women a superior class of people to whom men (especially minority men) may not speak. Someone who subscribes to androphobia is known as an androphobe.

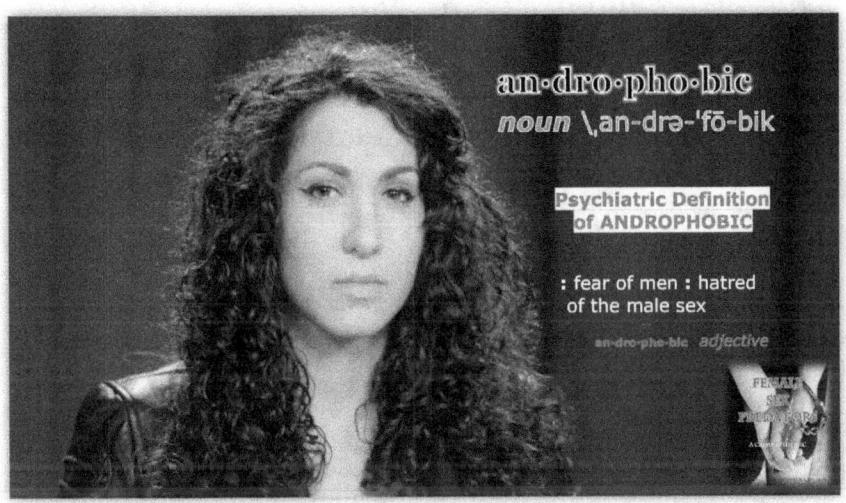

Another commentator, writing in U. S. A. Today, recognized how this type of misandrist (man-hating) propaganda is merely the "Jim Crow" South revisited in other areas of the U.S., and applied against all men, instead of just against African-American men.

The commentator, Glenn Reynolds, correctly noted that the video showed only Black men and Hispanic men "harassing" a white woman.

Where were the white guys? The video's producers said they just weren't able to get much good footage of them, for a variety of reasons. Whether, in the 10 hours of filming it took to produce their two-minute video, there just weren't enough white guys saying offensive stuff, or whether the producers just had bad luck or whether they edited out the white guys, the result was that they released a video about "street harassment" that was also, quite plainly, a video of minority men harassing a white woman. And whether or not it deserves the charges of outright racism and classism, or even comparisons to The Birth of a Nation, that it got from some minority critics, that's indisputably what it is.

Mr. Roberts continues in his commentary:

Second, and more troubling, the notion of going after minority males for inappropriate behavior toward white women raises unsettling memories of Jim Crow. Emmett Till, for example, a 14-year-old black youth who visited Mississippi from his home town of Chicago, broke the local behavioral code by flirting with a white cashier while buying some bubble gum. A few days later he was kidnapped, brutally beaten, and fatally shot in the head. An all-white jury, presumably viewing Till's behavior as culpable, refused to convict his killers.

I feel sure, of course, that the makers of today's catcalling video didn't think for a moment about the Emmett Till case, and I am positive that they would not endorse the fatal lynching of the men they pictured. Nonetheless, it's worth noting that the history of controlling minority men's intersexual behavior in this country is closely intertwined with the history of lynching. Those who choose to get involved in this field need to be aware of that history, lest they unintentionally make things worse.[14]

Mr. Reynolds' commentary raises some astute points about modern feminism, and its adoption of Klan principles.

The chivalry of the Klan was to elevate "white women" to semi-divine status. White women (but not minority women) were elevated to a status which conferred on them the right, and unfortunately the ability, to call forth the violence

---

[14] Glenn Harlan Reynolds, " Catcalling a two-way street," USA Today, November 10, 2014.
http://www.usatoday.com/story/opinion/2014/11/03/street-harassment-catcall-video-race-women-gender-equity-column/18373531/

of "white knights," based merely upon their own displeasure and accusations.

Modern feminists seek the same power with government violence. Modern feminists seek to be able to call for police arrests, incarceration, blackballing, censure and ruin of any man they choose to accuse based merely upon their displeasure. Modern feminism has done more to corrupt our current legal system, to erode due process rights of men (especially minority men), than any other corrupting influence in the United States or across the world.

In summary, although comparisons of rituals between the KKK and modern feminism may not be conclusive to establish their similarity, the substantive objectives of both movements are identical – they both seek to create a privileged class of white women, at the expense of oppressing men in general, and minority men in particular.

They are the same union.

John Davis, BA., J.D., LL.M.

Now Available

ABOUT THE AUTHOR

John Davis (1953 -) was born in Cleveland, Ohio. He was educated at Case Western Reserve University (BA) (one of the top ten universities in the United States), Seattle University School of Law (JD), and, New York University School of Law (LL.M post-doctoral) (one of the top ten law schools in the United States). John is fluent in seven languages (including ancient Latin and Greek). He has travelled the world over, many times, and has represented clients, in his thirty five year career, such as the United States Government and the Federation of Russia.

He has been a prosecutor three times in his 35 year career. He has held positions such as Assistant Attorney General (State of Arizona), United States Speaker, and Deputy District Attorney.

For most of his career in civil law, John was a successful international lawyer, practicing in many nations around the world.

John is now retired and lives in the South of France.